12-00

D1505829

Secret Weapons in the Civil War

Untold History of the Civil War

CHELSEA HOUSE PUBLISHERS

Untold History of the Civil War

Secret Weapons in the Civil War

Victor Brooks

CHELSEA HOUSE PUBLISHERS
Philadelphia

Produced by Combined Publishing
P.O. Box 307, Conshohocken, Pennsylvania 19428
1-800-418-6065
E-mail:combined@combinedpublishing.com
web:www.combinedpublishing.com

CHELSEA HOUSE PUBLISHERS

Editor in Chief: Stephen Reginald
Managing Editor: James D. Gallagher
Production Manager: Pamela Loos
Art Director: Sara Davis
Director of Photography: Judy L. Hasday
Senior Production Editor: LeeAnne Gelletly
Assistant Editor: Anne Hill

Front Cover Illustration: Courtesy of The Museum of the Confederacy, Richmond,
    Virginia; Photography by Katherine Wetzel

The Chelsea House World Wide Web site address is
http://www.chelseahouse.com

First Printing

135798642

Library of Congress Cataloging-in-Publication Data applied for:
ISBN 0-7910-5433-0

Contents

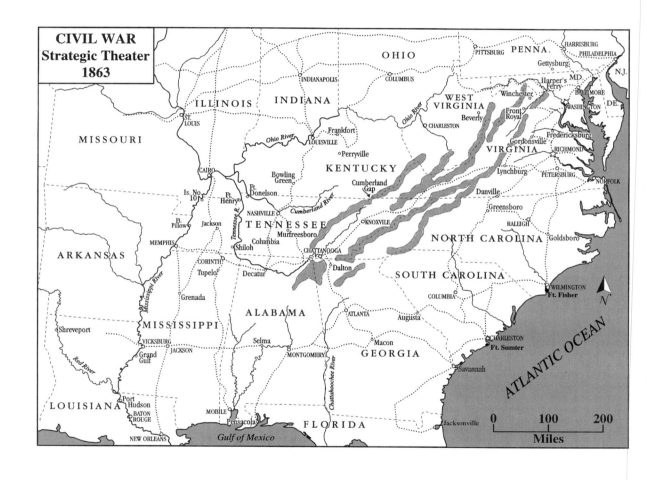

CIVIL WAR
Strategic Theater
1863

OHIO

ILLINOIS

INDIANA

PITTSBURG   PENNA.
HARRISBURG
PHILADELPHIA
Gettysburg
N.J.
Harper's
Ferry   MD.
Winchester   BALTIMORE
WEST
VIRGINIA   Front   WASHINGTON   DE.
Royal
Beverly
CHARLESTON

INDIANAPOLIS
COLUMBUS

MISSOURI

ST.
LOUIS

Ohio River
Frankfort
LOUISVILLE

Ohio River
CHARLESTON

Gordonsville   Fredericksburg
VIRGINIA   RICHMOND

CAIRO

Perryville

KENTUCKY

Lynchburg   PETERSBURG
Danville   NORFOLK

Is. No.
10
Ft.
Henry

Bowling
Green
Ft.
Donelson

Cumberland
Gap

Greensboro

Pillow
Jackson

NASHVILLE
Cumberland River

KNOXVILE

RALEIGH

MEMPHIS

Columbia
Murfreesboro
TENNESSEE

NORTH CAROLINA   Goldsboro

ARKANSAS

CORINTH
Tupelo
Decatur

Shiloh
CHATTANOOGA

Dalton

SOUTH CAROLINA

WILMINGTON
Ft. Fisher

Grenada

ALABAMA

ATLANTA
Augusta

COLUMBIA

N

Shreveport

MISSISSIPPI

Selma

Macon
GEORGIA

CHARLESTON
Ft. Sumter

VICKSBURG
JACKSON
Grand
Gulf

MONTGOMERY

Savannah

ATLANTIC OCEAN

LOUISIANA   Port
Hudson
BATON
ROUGE

MOBILE

Pensacola

FLORIDA

Jacksonville

0   100   200

NEW ORLEANS   Gulf of Mexico

Miles

**CIVIL WAR
IN THE EAST**

Virginia & Maryland

N

10 Miles

Sharpsburg
Frederick

Harper's
Ferry

BALTIMORE

Winchester

Potomac R.

District of
Columbia

Shanandoah Mountains

Shanandoah Valley

Thoroughfare Gap

WASHINGTON

Rectortown

Front Royal

Alexandria

Blue Ridge Mtns.

Manassas Jct.

Bristoe Sta.

New
Market

Rappahannock Sta

Culpepper

Aquia Cr.

Rapidan R.

Falmouth

Potomac R.

Chancellorsville

Fredericksburg

Staunton

Spotsylvania

Gordonsville

N. Anna R.

S. Anna R.

Rappahannock R.

Mattapony R.

Chesapeake Bay

Pamunkey R.

Mechanicsville

Gaines
Mill

Cold
Harbor

Seven
Pines

RICHMOND

Chickahominy R.

York R.

Malvern Hill

Appomattox
C.H.

Appomattox R.

Bermuda
Hundred

Harrison's
Landing

Yorktown

PETERSBURG

Williamsburg

James R.

Fort Monroe

Norfolk

Gosport Navy
Yard

7

Civil War Chronology

1860

November 6   Abraham Lincoln is elected president of the United States.

December 20   South Carolina becomes the first state to secede from the Union.

1861

January-April   Mississippi, Florida, Alabama, Georgia, Louisiana, and Texas also secede from the Union.

April 1   Bombardment of Fort Sumter begins the Civil War.

April-May   Lincoln calls for volunteers to fight the Southern rebellion, causing a second wave of secession with Virginia, Arkansas, Tennessee, and North Carolina all leaving the Union.

May   Union naval forces begin blockading the Confederate coast and reoccupying some Southern ports and offshore islands.

July 21   Union forces are defeated at the battle of First Bull Run and withdraw to Washington.

1862

February   Previously unknown Union general Ulysses S. Grant captures Confederate garrisons in Tennessee at Fort Henry (February 6) and Fort Donelson (February 16).

March 7-8   Confederates and their Cherokee allies are defeated at Pea Ridge, Arkansas.

March 8-9   Naval battle at Hampton Roads, Virginia, involving the USS *Monitor* and the CSS *Virginia* (formerly the USS *Merrimac*) begins the era of the armored fighting ship.

April-July   The Union army marches on Richmond after an amphibious landing. Confederate forces block Northern advance in a series of battles. Robert E. Lee is placed in command of the main Confederate army in Virginia.

April 6-7   Grant defeats the Southern army at Shiloh Church, Tennessee, after a costly two-day battle.

April 27   New Orleans is captured by Union naval forces under Admiral David Farragut.

May 31   The battle of Seven Pines (also called Fair Oaks) is fought and the Union lines are held.

August 29-30   Lee wins substantial victory over the Army of the Potomac at the battle of Second Bull Run near Manassas, Virginia.

September 17   Union General George B. McClellan repulses Lee's first invasion of the North at Antietam Creek near Sharpsburg, Maryland, in the bloodiest single day of the war.

November 13   Grant begins operations against the key Confederate fortress at Vicksburg, Mississippi.

December 13   Union forces suffer heavy losses storming Confederate positions at Fredericksburg, Virginia.

1863

January 1   President Lincoln issues the Emancipation Proclamation, freeing the slaves in the Southern states.

May 1-6	Lee wins an impressive victory at Chancellorsville, but key Southern commander Thomas J. "Stonewall" Jackson dies of wounds, an irreplaceable loss for the Army of Northern Virginia.
June	The city of Vicksburg and the town of Port Hudson are held under siege by the Union army. They surrender on July 4.
July 1-3	Lee's second invasion of the North is decisively defeated at Gettysburg, Pennsylvania.
July 16	Union forces led by the black 54th Massachusetts Infantry attempt to regain control of Fort Sumter by attacking the Fort Wagner outpost.
September 19-20	Confederate victory at Chickamauga, Georgia, gives some hope to the South after disasters at Gettysburg and Vicksburg.

1864

February 17	A new Confederate submarine, the *Hunley,* attacks and sinks the USS *Housatonic* in the waters off Charleston.
March 9	General Grant is made supreme Union commander. He decides to campaign in the East with the Army of the Potomac while General William T. Sherman carries out a destructive march across the South from the Mississippi to the Atlantic coast.
May-June	In a series of costly battles (Wilderness, Spotsylvania, and Cold Harbor), Grant gradually encircles Lee's troops in the town of Petersburg, Richmond's railway link to the rest of the South.
June 19	The siege of Petersburg begins, lasting for nearly a year until the end of the war.
August 27	General Sherman captures Atlanta and begins the "March to the Sea," a campaign of destruction across Georgia and South Carolina.
November 8	Abraham Lincoln wins reelection, ending hope of the South getting a negotiated settlement.
November 30	Confederate forces are defeated at Franklin, Tennessee, losing five generals. Nashville is soon captured (December 15-16).

1865

April 2	Major Petersburg fortifications fall to the Union, making further resistance by Richmond impossible.
April 3-8	Lee withdraws his army from Richmond and attempts to reach Confederate forces still holding out in North Carolina. Union armies under Grant and Sheridan gradually encircle him.
April 9	Lee surrenders to Grant at Appomattox, Virginia, effectively ending the war.
April 14	Abraham Lincoln is assassinated by John Wilkes Booth, a Southern sympathizer.

Union Army
Army of the Potomac
Army of the James
Army of the Cumberland

Confederate Army
Army of Northern Virginia
Army of Tennessee

I

Yankee Ingenuity

On a warm, late winter day in 1861, the tiny Federal garrison defending Fort Sumter was involved in one of the strangest Washington's Birthday celebrations in American history. Major Robert Anderson ordered his blue-coated gunners to fire a 13-gun salute to honor the nation's first president. However, the men defending this unfinished fort in Charleston Harbor were now technically foreigners in South Carolina as that state and six other southern states had recently voted to secede from the Union and form their own Confederate States of America. Yet, for one brief moment the rising hostility between Northerners and Southerners was suspended. As the 13 cannon shots echoed through the balmy air, the Confederate-held positions ringing Fort Sumter answered with their own enthusiastic salutes to a man who was still a hero in both North and South.

Despite the temporary goodwill of that single afternoon, Major Anderson knew that he had only about 70 men available to face a Confederate army of almost

Some of the barrels at Fort Sumter were filled with cannonballs and stones to make a new weapon—flying fougasses.

7,000 men deployed around Charleston Harbor. He therefore asked his officers to begin suggesting innovative weapons that might even the odds in case of an all-out attack. Lieutenant Thomas Seymour, a bright young artillery officer, surveyed the materials in the fort and quickly constructed the first "secret weapon" of the Civil War, a device called the "flying fougasse." Lieutenant Seymour's plan was to place a cannonball in the center of a barrel filled with paving stones. When the barrel was rolled off one of Sumter's walls, it would explode and spray stones in all directions. A few days later Seymour tried out his new weapon and all around Charleston Harbor Southern civilians and soldiers watched the terrifying demonstration. A Charleston newspaper called the new Yankee weapon "a devastating infernal machine that seemed to have enormous destructive possibilities." Soon these deadly barrels were stacked along Sumter's stone walls, early versions of hand grenades were placed in key positions, and Sumter's small wharf was rigged with explosives that could be triggered from a safe distance away.

While Fort Sumter surrendered before any of these new weapons could be used, the first confrontation between North and South provided a preview of the ingenuity that Yankees and Rebels would use in developing new weapons to swing the tide of war in their favor. This book will look at several of these exciting yet terrifying weapons that helped make the Civil War the first truly "modern" war in history.

II

The Rifle War

The surrender of Fort Sumter forced both Federal and Confederate governments to begin recruiting armies larger than anything that had ever been seen in America. Most of these new recruits would be armed with the most common weapon of the time, a single-shot musket. The earlier version of this gun was called a smoothbore musket because it had a barrel with a smooth surface on the inside while the more modern version was called a rifled musket because it contained grooves or "rifling" in the barrel that propelled the bullet several times as far as the smoothbore. One of the major problems that faced men who were armed with these muskets was that they were muzzleloaders, that is, the soldier had to ram the bullet down the front of a very long barrel, a process that usually had to be done while you were standing upright. Not only could you only reload the gun two or three times a minute, you were often a perfect target for an enemy soldier. By the beginning of the Civil War, a number of inventors had developed a much

THE RIFLE WAR

Rifles were the primary weapon of the Civil War. Here Private Edmund Ruffin, the Confederate soldier who fired the first shot against Fort Sumter, poses with his rifle.

better weapon called a breechloader which would fire much faster and allow a soldier to load bullets in the rear of the weapon. This remarkable new weapon promised to not only give soldiers more firepower, but would let them load their guns while crouched behind a fence or wall or even when they were lying on the ground.

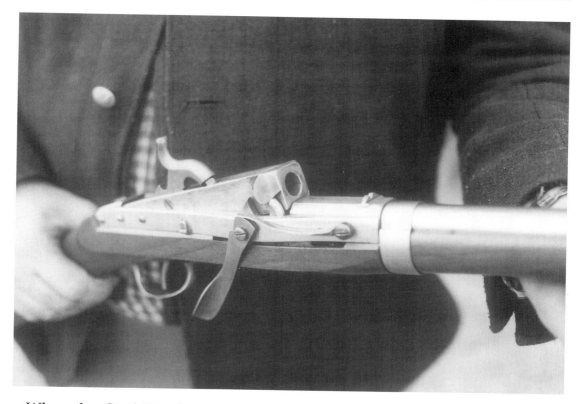

When the Civil War began, the Union had a huge advantage in the rifle war over the Confederacy because the North had almost all of the factories that could build breech-loading rifles. However, instead of the Yankee soldiers marching into the early battles with these new guns, most of the bluecoats fought much of the war armed with the same muzzleloaders as their graycoat opponents. There were several reasons why the North took quite awhile to provide its soldiers with really modern weapons.

The first major problem was that arsenals and storehouses around the North were filled with over a half-million muskets that were gathering dust and taking up space. When Union officials realized that they were going to have to raise a huge army, they immediately turned to this enormous backlog of spare weapons.

The new breech-loading rifle allowed the soldiers to load their guns more safely and easily.

Colonel Hiram Berdan formed a regiment of sharpshooters for the Union Army.

War Department officials also knew that even when this large supply of muskets ran out, they could make new muskets for about $10 each while breechloaders would cost between $30 and $100. Another problem slowing down a switch over to breechloaders was the challenge of providing enough ammunition to soldiers in a battle. Civil War soldiers usually went into a battle carrying between 40 and 60 bullets for their muskets. Since the Union army often could put around 100,000 men into a battle, this meant that supply officers would have to provide their men with between 4 million and 6 million bullets just to start the battle. Even a soldier armed with a muzzleloader could fire all of the ammunition he carried in about a half hour of serious fighting, and at that point, supply wagons would have to begin bringing up huge reserve stockpiles of bullets. Since breech-loading rifles could often be fired five or even ten times as fast as a musket, supply experts became very alarmed at the thought of their soldiers using their whole supply of ammunition in only two or three minutes of fighting. General Winfield Scott, the crotchety, brusque, 75-year-old commander of the Federal army at the beginning of the war probably best summarized many traditional attitudes toward new weapons. He insisted, "the muzzleloader is, has been, and always will be the American soldier's prime weapon. Breechloaders would spoil our troops by allowing them to fire too fast and will encourage them to waste ammunition."

While many senior generals preferred to go to war with guns that couldn't fire any faster than in George

Washington's time, a growing number of lower-ranking officers became determined to arm their men with the most modern weapons available. During the Civil War, any person who had the energy, and money, to recruit 1,000 volunteers was allowed to form those men into a regiment which he would command. He was also given considerable freedom to choose the uniforms and weapons for those men, especially if he didn't ask the government to pay for those items. One good example of this ability to be innovative is the experience of Colonel Hiram Berdan. When the Civil War began, Berdan was the owner of a prosperous New York City engineering firm. Berdan had married into a very rich family, had a number of wealthy friends, and yet very much wanted to fight to save the Union. Rather than concentrating on recruiting New York City men to form a new regiment, Berdan con-

One of Berdan's sharpshooters waits in ambush for the Rebel army. Berdan's sharpshooters used the new Sharps breech-loading rifles.

ducted a well-publicized contest to raise a national regiment of outstanding sharpshooters who would form one of the most elite units in the Union army. Tryouts were held across the country and to even survive the first cut a candidate had to put 10 consecutive shots into a target at 200 yards with no shot to be more than two inches from the center of the bulls-eye. The regional shoot-offs attracted great attention, including the interest of President Lincoln, and soon 1,000 winners were enlisted in the 1st United States Sharpshooters.

Berdan outfitted his men in green uniforms that would be difficult to see in wooded areas and then equipped his men with the Colt company's new 50-caliber Sharps, open-sight, breech-loading rifle. Berdan gained presidential support for his regiment when he staged a spectacular mock battle and shootout on the White House lawn, and by the early summer of 1863 companies of sharpshooters were serving throughout the Army of the Potomac. However, until the battle of Gettysburg, most of the sharpshooters had been parceled out in squads of 10 or 12 men and not even a full company had ever been fully engaged in a battle that would test their abilities. Finally, on July 2, 1863, during the second day of the battle of Gettysburg, Berdan had his chance to show what his men could do.

While new Army of the Potomac commander General George Meade and his Third Corps commander, General Daniel Sickles, bickered angrily over where the main Confederate attack of the day might strike, Colonel Berdan was ordered to take 100 of his sharpshooters and scout the Emmitsburg Road to detect any sign of a rebel advance from that direction. Berdan deployed his green-clad soldiers along the heavily wooded banks of Pitzer's Creek and told his men to line up 40 cartridges next to their guns. A short time later, as the sharpshooters peered expectantly across the other side of the creek, they spotted the spearhead of the 10th and 11th Alabama Regiments pushing through the thickets in the torrid summer afternoon heat. Suddenly, Berdan's right hand slashed down and a solid sheet of flame erupted from the wooded bank. The Confederates in the creek were blasted back as if swept by an invisible scythe and the orderly advance became chaos. As the shrieks of wounded men mingled with the shouts of startled officers, the whole timetable of the Rebel advance was shattered. The water turned crimson, choked with the bodies of fallen graycoats as the sharpshooters kept up a steady and murderous fire. In an engagement that even Confederate First Corps commander James Longstreet called "a clever fight," Berdan lost 19 men and 24 were wounded, but they repelled a much larger force of Confederates for a crucial 20 minutes. Although the sharpshooters were finally forced to retreat when their ammunition was exhausted, it took the Rebels another 20 minutes to regroup and reorganize, a delay which gave valuable time for the Union defenders to rush reinforcements to critical points on their line.

During the fighting that followed that afternoon, General Sickles lost a leg, but from his hospital bed he wrote Colonel Berdan, "the action at Pitzer's Creek deserves to be inscribed on your battleflag. It was a brilliant feat of arms, of inestimable advantage to the decisive victory of July 2, from which the enemy never recovered." By bloody demonstration, the battle in Pitzer's Woods showed that a few men armed with breechloaders could be more than a match for a far larger force armed with old-fashioned muzzleloaders.

As the war continued, this lesson would be learned more and more often.

Berdan's sharpshooters had entered battle with the first generation of breechloaders, rifles that would be loaded one bullet at a time. However, a second generation of breechloaders called magazine rifles would prove even more deadly to Confederate opponents. These new guns, such as Spencer and Henry repeating rifles, were designed to carry preloaded magazines of 7 to 15 bullets which could be inserted into the rear of the gun and then fired very quickly. Awestruck Confederate soldiers called these new weapons "the Yankee guns that you load on Sunday and fire all week," and these new rifles soon had a major effect on the battlefield.

Because the Spencer and Henry repeating rifles usually could not shoot as far as the Springfield muskets, the new guns were first issued to cavalry units that tended to fight in much closer quarters than infantry. However, by the fall of 1863 a Union general named John Wilder had specially trained and equipped a brigade of men who rode horses and carried repeating rifles but would be used as infantry when they reached the battlefield. In September of 1863 this new type of unit proved its worth at the bloody battle of Chickamaugua. Wilder's brigade was part of General William Rosecrans's Federal army which had just captured Chattanooga and was pushing into northern Georgia when Confederate General Braxton Bragg's Army of Tennessee, reinforced by General Longstreet's corps of the Army of Northern Virginia, smashed into the Yankees. This was one of the few battles in the Civil War where the Rebels had more men on the field than the Federals, and at a crucial moment in the fighting almost 16,000 graycoats smashed through a hole in the Union lines and threat-

This captain in the 7th Illinois Infantry holds a Henry repeating rifle.

ened to cut the Northern army in two. At this moment, Wilder's 1,600 men emerged from a dense line of trees and poured a deadly stream of repeating-rifle fire into the startled Confederates. This important action gave most of the rest of the bluecoats time to retreat and avoid an even worse disaster.

A year later, the new commander of the Confederate Army of Tennessee, General John Bell Hood, faced an even larger force of men armed with repeating rifles. Hood ordered one of the most spectacular charges of the Civil War against a Union army defending the town of Franklin, Tennessee, in December of 1864. As dozens of Confederate bands played during a sunny but short afternoon, thousands of gray-coated soldiers sounded the Rebel yell and charged at the Yankee defenses around the Carter House. However, a large number of the bluecoats defending the area around the house were armed with repeating rifles and their awesome firepower simply tore the surging Southern line to pieces. In this part of the battlefield, the Confederates lost 10 men killed for every Yankee who died and several of the bravest Southern generals in their army died in the murderous wall of fire. As the Confederacy neared the end of its existence, it became clear to both Northerners and Southerners that future wars would be fought by the powerful new rifles that were being introduced on Civil War battlefields.

III

The Ironclad War

On the warm, spring evening of April 19, 1861, over 800 sailors and marines of the United States Navy prepared to evacuate the huge Gosport Navy Yard near Norfolk. Only hours earlier, the state of Virginia had decided to secede from the Union and join the new Confederacy, and it would be only a matter of time until the Rebels seized this valuable base. Commodore Charles McCauley, the elderly, 68-year-old commander of Gosport, was panic-stricken about the Virginians getting their hands on the hundreds of cannons, tons of naval supplies, and nine ships that would be the main prizes when the base was captured. Therefore, he ordered a huge demolition operation in which cannons and storehouses were blown up and the fleet of ships was burned. A few hours after the bluecoats had evacuated the burning naval yard, Virginia militia units marched in and discovered that the most valuable ship in Gosport, the powerful steam frigate USS *Merrimack*, had been only partially

The battle between the CSS Virginia *and the USS* Monitor *at Hampton Roads, Virginia, began the war of the ironclads.*

destroyed and might be rebuilt as an addition to the new Confederate navy.

At the beginning of the Civil War, major changes were underway in the operation of ships. Until a few decades earlier, ships were almost always made of wood and used sails to move on the water. However, Robert Fulton's development of the steamboat combined with the ability of new factories to manufacture large amounts of iron plating meant that very new kinds of ships might be on the horizon. Political leaders and naval officials in both the North and the South quickly understood these changes, but the Confederates were just a little ahead of the Yankees in turning their ideas into real ships. The Confederate secretary of the navy, Floridian Stephen Mallory, realized that his infant service could never challenge the established Federal navy ship for ship. Therefore, Mallory insisted to the Confederate Congress that "I regard the possession of an iron-armored ship as a matter of the first necessity," and convinced the government to finance a reconstruction of the captured *Merrimack*.

During the winter of 1861-1862 the *Merrimack* was plugged, pumped out, raised, salty mud swabbed out of her engines, and her damaged hull cut nearly to the water's edge. While some workers attached a four-foot-long iron ram to her prow, others built a slope-walled housing for her guns and crew. Ten large guns were specially reinforced with iron hoops that would allow them to fire extra-powerful powder charges and then were fitted into embrasures. Then workers covered the *Merrimack* all over, down to two feet below the waterline, with overlapping plates of two-inch armor rolled from railroad iron. By March of 1862 the powerful new ironclad, renamed the CSS *Virginia*, was ready for action.

On March 8, Commodore Franklin Buchanan ordered the *Virginia* to steam out from Norfolk and head toward the Union naval squadron guarding the mouth of the James River at the channel called Hampton Roads. The Federal blockade force included the *Merrimack*'s two sister ships, the steam frigates *Minnesota* and *Roanoke*, as well as three sailing vessels, the 50-gun frigates *St. Lawrence* and *Congress* and the 30-gun sloop *Cumberland*. As all of the Federal ships fired furiously "having no more effect than peas from a pop-gun," the Confederate ironclad sent several shells into the Union sloop and then tore a gaping seven-foot hole in her hull with her ram. The

The Roanoke *(above) was saved from destruction by the arrival of the new Northern ironclad, the* Monitor.

Cumberland quickly sank to the bottom of Hampton Roads, taking half of her crew with her, and the *Virginia* then smashed the *Congress* into helpless driftwood, an action that killed Buchanan's brother who was an officer on the Federal ship. Even worse, when the *Minnesota* and the *Roanoke* steamed up to help the sailing ships, they both grounded on sandbars and seemed doomed to share the same fate. However, Commodore Buchanan had been wounded in the battle, the *Virginia* was low on fuel, and it seemed likely that the Yankee ships would be just as easy to destroy the next morning.

March 9, 1862, dawned clear and cold and Lieutenant Catsby-Jones, Buchanan's successor in command of the *Virginia*, eagerly awaited the annihilation of the whole Union blockade squadron. But as the Confederate ship moved in close to finish off the *Minnesota*, the Rebel sailors noticed a strange-looking vessel sitting beside the Yankee frigate. At first they thought they were seeing a raft that was preparing to take off the ship's engines in order to refloat the vessel, but as they drew closer they realized that

this strange looking little "raft" was equipped with cannons.

The vessel that Catsby-Jones and his men saw perched near the *Minnesota* was in some respects even more revolutionary than the *Virginia*. The name of this Northern ship was the *Monitor* and it had been developed specifically to challenge the Rebel ironclad. When Union spies had reported the reconstruction of the *Merrimack*, Union secretary of the navy Gideon Welles and President Abraham Lincoln had agreed that the North must match this new Rebel secret weapon. Welles, whom Lincoln called "Father Neptune," contracted with cantankerous, eccentric, Swedish naval engineer John Ericsson to design an ironclad ship that could counteract the *Virginia*. Ericsson started three months later than the Southern builders, but was actually able to launch the *Monitor* a little ahead of the Confederate ironclad. The completed ship was built so close to water level that people called it "a cheese box on a raft" or "a tin can on a shingle," but the small size of the vessel made it almost impossible to hit. The *Monitor* was fitted out

The CSS Virginia *drawn by an officer on the* Roanoke. *The* Virginia *was actually a rebuilt Union vessel, the* Merrimack.

Lieutenant John Worden, commander of the USS Monitor, *was wounded in the famous battle with the CSS* Virginia.

with armor between five and nine inches thick and armed with two incredibly powerful 11-inch rifled cannons housed in a revolutionary revolving turret that gave the craft the firepower of a ship with many times more guns. Now, still technically on a "shakedown cruise" after her launching, the *Monitor* was preparing to prevent the *Virginia* from demolishing an entire Union naval squadron.

As the *Virginia* maneuvered to ram the *Minnesota*, Lieutenant John Worden, captain of the *Monitor*, ordered his ship to steam out and engage the Confederate ship. The Rebels turned their attention to the strange-looking little ironclad and fired a broad-

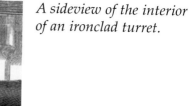

A sideview of the interior of an ironclad turret.

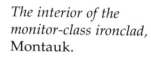

The interior of the monitor-class ironclad, Montauk.

side which simply bounced off the *Monitor*'s incredibly thick armor. The *Monitor* was actually hit 23 times by the *Virginia*'s guns but the only significant damage occurred when a shell struck the ship's pilot house and wounded Worden. The Union ironclad's much more powerful guns scored almost 50 hits on the *Virginia* and managed to crack the Rebel ship's outer plating at several places. However, after almost four hours of sparring with one another, the crews of both ships were exhausted and, almost by mutual consent, the two ironclads disengaged with each side con-

The powerful ironclad, the CSS Tennessee *battles the U.S. steamer* Richmond. *The* Tennessee *was the South's most powerful ironclad.*

vinced that they had won the duel. The day of masts, sails, and wood in navel vessels was clearly almost finished and when the news of this historic battle reached England, the London *Times* insisted that except for two experimental British ironclads, "there is now not a ship in the English navy that it would not be madness to trust to an engagement with that little *Monitor*."

While the *Virginia-Monitor* duel began the war of ironclads, within two years each side had more and bigger armored ships fighting in a series of desperate battles from the Atlantic Ocean to the Gulf of Mexico.

On August 5, 1864, as Admiral David Farragut took 18 Union ships past the Confederate forts guarding the enormously important port of Mobile, Alabama, the Rebel navy countered with the most powerful of the second generation of Southern ironclads, the CSS *Tennessee*. One of the four monitor-class Union ironclads accompanying Admiral Farragut blew up when the ship sailed into a Confederate minefield, but the remaining three ironclads played a huge role in the ultimate Federal victory. The *Tennessee* was covered with six-inch armorplating and had nearly twice the fire power of the *Virginia*, but she still faced a squadron of enemy ironclads backed up by more conventional vessels that were now fitted out with protective armor themselves. In a stunning preview of 20th-century naval fleet action, the *Tennessee* and her escorts were pounded into submission and a whole new era of naval warfare was confirmed.

A Rebel ram vessel, used to blow up large ships by ramming them with explosives.

IV

The Undersea War

*O*n a still, humid evening in July of 1861, one of the most energetic officers in the new Confederate States Navy set out in a small rowboat to launch a daring attack on Yankee warships near Norfolk, Virginia. Commander Matthew Maury had been considered one of the most ingenious officers in the United States fleet and the new Southern navy quickly put him in charge of harbor defenses for the Confederacy. Since the Rebels did not yet have any major ships of their own to challenge the Federal ships beginning to blockade ports, Maury decided that the best way to fight the Yankees was by using newly developed electric mines that could be launched from very small boats.

Commander Maury was eager to try out this awesome new weapon himself, and on a moonless night in this first summer of the war, he set out at the head of five rowboats, each equipped with an electric mine. The tiny craft closed in on the Union frigates *Minnesota* and *Roanoke*, and Maury breathed a sigh of relief when he noticed that the Yankees had posted

Commander Matthew Maury made a daring attack from five rowboats on the Union frigates in the waters off Virginia.

few lookouts to warn of an attack. The commander and his men quickly unloaded powder kegs equipped with complex trigger mechanisms and quietly floated them toward the two Federal ships. Each of the weapons drifted very close to the targets and moments later Maury whispered a command to set off the mines. But as the barrels had drifted toward the Union ships, the detonating mechanisms had been jarred loose and when the triggers were set off there was only deathly silence. If the weapons had worked, both Federal ships would have been badly damaged, but Maury and his men would have been killed as well, for in the excitement, the Confederates had moved so close to their prey that they would have been obliterated by the explosion. Maury now slipped back toward Confederate territory and immediately began thinking of more reliable ways to attack the Yankees from under the sea.

The most daring idea in undersea warfare was to attempt to build a boat that could submerge and attack an enemy without being seen. During the War of Independence, a young American patriot by the name of David Bushnell had actually built a primitive, one-man submarine called the *Turtle*. When the British stationed a huge war fleet near New York City in the summer of 1776, Bushnell had maneuvered the *Turtle* near the Royal Navy warship *Eagle* and tried to attach an explosive device to the ship's hull. While the

American ran out of air before he could fully attach the weapon, his exploit was well-publicized and naval leaders of the Civil War were convinced that they could succeed where Bushnell had failed.

The Federal navy did not ignore the possibility of submarine warfare, but it was the Confederate navy, which was outnumbered badly in conventional ships, that put the most energy into undersea operations. By the summer of 1863, as the Yankee blockade of Southern harbors began to tighten rapidly, Confederate engineers had developed a powerful counterweapon called the *David*. The *Davids* were constructed from the shells of old gunboats that were cut down close to the waterline, covered with iron plat-

A Confederate torpedo boat, the David, *aground at Charleston, N.C. The* Davids *were small vessels equipped to ram larger vessels with explosives.*

ing, and armed with 100-pound charges of gunpowder fixed to the end of a long spar at the bow. The plan was to ram a Union vessel hard enough so that the spar would stick like a spear, then back off 100 feet and set off the explosive by yanking a long cord attached to the detonator. The first few *David* attacks were disasters as the charges either went off too early or the Federals spotted the boats before they could get close enough to ram. However, during the night of October 5, 1863, a *David* was sent out against the powerful Union steam frigate *New Ironsides*. The explosive was driven into the Yankee ship's hull, the Rebel boat backed off and set off the charge. As a result of the explosion that followed, the Federal warship was ripped open so badly that it was out of action for months.

Once this kind of attack proved it could work, Confederate naval officials and engineers began thinking about how to attack the Yankees from beneath the water rather than on the surface. A southern inventor by the name of Horace Hunley soon came up with a plan for a dramatically upgraded version of Bushnell's *Turtle*. The new vessel was constructed from a 25-foot section of iron boiler, four feet wide and six feet deep. Both bow and stern were pointed and each end contained a ballast tank, which could be filled to make the boat submerge and pumped out to make it rise to the surface. On the top was a small conning tower which protruded about a foot above the waterline. Using four tiny glass observation ports in this tower, the captain could see where he was going and direct the activities of eight crewmen who would sit inside the boat and turn a crankshaft with their arms. The shaft was attached to a propeller at the stern. The plan was to approach an enemy ship at night, plunge a spar into the hull, back off, and fire the explosive device. At this point, the submarine would submerge and pull safely away.

The first "shakedown cruises" of the radical new boat were all total disasters. Three times the submarine attempted to submerge and each time the crew was unable to make the boat return to the surface. Three entire crews, one including Horace Hunley, had been drowned. But the Confederate officers decided to send the submarine on a mission anyway, one which did not seem to be any more dangerous than her sea trials. On the clear chilly night of February 17, 1864, the submarine, now named the *Hunley* in honor of its inventor, slowly moved out of Breach Inlet near Charleston Harbor and inched toward open water. Lieutenant George Dixon, the *Hunley*'s latest commander, carefully maneuvered his tiny boat toward the Union warship *Housatonic* and began the tricky operation of flooding the bow and stern tanks. A few minutes later the *Hunley* was submerged and by 9 P.M. it had closed to within a few feet of the Yankee ship. While bluecoat sailors turned out in alarm when they heard a strange thud hit the hull, Dixon backed off and ignited the demolition charge. Seconds later, an enormous explosion sent streaks of flame into the cold night sky and panic-stricken sailors climbed down the sides of the rapidly sinking Yankee vessel. In only four minutes, the *Housatonic* was at the bottom of the harbor, but Dixon and his men never had a chance to celebrate—the *Hunley* had not pulled back far enough from the *Housatonic* and the Union ship took its enemy to the bottom with it. Despite the loss of the *Hunley*, Confederates cheered the first successful submarine attack in history.

The sinking of the *Housatonic* shocked most people in the North, but a few months later the Yankees would have a large measure of revenge. During the

The Confederate **Albermarle**, *one of the most imposing of the Rebel ships plagued the Union ships anchored in Albermarle Sound.*

summer of 1864 the Confederates challenged Union operations along the coast of North Carolina with one of the most powerful ships of its time, the new iron-clad *Albermarle*. This imposing vessel would sweep up and down Albermarle Sound pounding Union ships and shore batteries and then steam back to an almost impenetrable base guarded by floating walls of logs. Finally, after every attempt to sink the *Albermarle* had failed, Lieutenant William Cushing, a young Union naval officer, proposed a daring plan that would give the Rebels a taste of their own medicine in torpedo warfare. Cushing received direct support from Secretary of the Navy Gideon Welles, and he hand-picked a crew of 14 volunteers who would sail a small steamcutter up to the *Albermarle*'s base during the night, and then destroy her with a torpedo very much like the one the *Hunley* had used on the *Housatonic*.

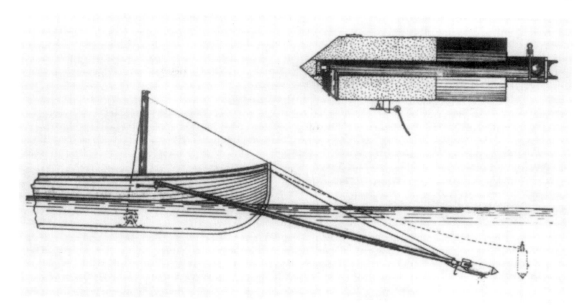

Just after sunset on October 26, 1864, the 15 bluecoats began an eight-mile run into Albermarle Sound and then closed on the huge Rebel ironclad which Cushing insisted looked like "a mountain of iron." Suddenly, the Union cutter was detected by Confederate lookouts on the shore, and a combination of land-based cannons and the *Albermarle*'s powerful guns started pounding the Yankee ship which was now silhouetted against blazing bonfires. While Cushing's single cannon dueled with the Rebel batteries, the young Yankee officer spotted a weak spot in the log barrier and rammed the cutter through until it was beside the *Albermarle*. With enormous luck, Cushing found a vulnerable spot in the ship's armorplating, plunged the torpedo into the hull, and released the firing pin. A series of explosions ripped through the *Albermarle* just as Rebel batteries were turning the Union ship into driftwood. Cushing yelled "abandon ship!" and went over the side into the frigid water while the rest of his crew was wiped out in the explosion. The young

A side view of Cushing's spar torpedo showing how it was used to ram a ship under water.

Annapolis graduate swam to the nearest shore, avoided Confederate patrols, and at dawn staggered into Union lines to become the center of attention from President Lincoln on down. Now both North and South had proved that weapons that could be used below the waves could be just as deadly as the cannons that were fired on the surface.

V

The Air War

Just as the Civil War added a new dimension to warfare with the first successful use of underwater weapons, the war between North and South also pushed combat operations into the skies. When the first hot air balloons were launched in the late 18th century, Benjamin Franklin had suggested using balloons as troop carriers for an invasion of an enemy country. During the Mexican War a balloonist named John Wise insisted that the United States Army could use balloons to drop bombs on Vera Cruz to support the American invasion of Mexico. However, it would take the outbreak of fighting between the Union and the Confederacy to prove that an aerial dimension to warfare was more than fantasy.

While Abraham Lincoln and his first general, George B. McClellan, would end up disagreeing on almost everything about how to fight the Rebels, they were both enthusiastic about developing an aeronautical force for the Union army. The two men were enthusiastic about a balloon corps mainly due to the

Professor Lowe takes off in one of his observation balloons that greatly aided Union strategy.

energy and personality of a 31-year-old aeronaut named Thaddeus Lowe. Professor Lowe had spent most of the 1850s developing the new science of aeronautics, and by 1861 was fascinated about the possibilities of trans-Atlantic balloon travel. However, the outbreak of hostilities shifted his priorities and he headed to Washington to promote the idea of a balloon corps to help the Union win the war.

When Lowe arrived in the capital, the Federal army was already experimenting with observation balloons.

However, because the airships were powered by huge steam engines it was almost impossible to move them with an advancing army. Also, the signal flags the aeronauts carried were hard to read far below on the ground so the information they discovered could not be used until the balloon had landed. Lowe came to Washington with solutions to both of these problems. First, he had just perfected a major invention, a portable hydrogen generator that could be transported anywhere on a battlefield. Second, he proposed installing telegraph sets in the balloons which would allow instant transmission of information back to army headquarters during a battle.

Lowe used a number of political connections to gain a dinner invitation from Abraham Lincoln, and by the end of the meal the aeronaut had received presidential backing for an experimental operation. On the sunny, hot afternoon of June 18, 1861, Lowe took off in the balloon *Enterprise* from the Washington Armory and flew directly over the White House. A few minutes later the aeronaut was aiming a telescope at the military encampments and fortifications around the capital. He then sent a cable to President Lincoln describing all of the key features of the forts while insisting that he could see clearly over a 50-mile radius. He then wired the president, "I have pleasure in sending you the first dispatch ever sent from an aerial station and acknowledge my indebtedness for the opportunity of demonstrating the availability of the science of aeronautics in the service of the country." For over an hour, the *Enterprise* hovered in the humid, hazy, summer sky while Lowe flashed messages to military bases as far away as Philadelphia. When the aeronaut landed, he received a message from Lincoln instructing him to make the White House lawn his new temporary ground base so that the president could personally watch the drama of the balloon ascents.

A few days later, the *Enterprise* was used for its first full-scale military mission. On June 22 rumors reached the Federal capital that a large Confederate army was massing 30 miles to the south in preparation for an attack on Washington. Lowe was assigned to the mission of confirming the Rebel intentions and he flew well into Virginia to scout the enemy. The aeronaut saw no major Southern forces close enough to be an immediate menace to Washington, but when he drifted over enemy-held Fairfax Courthouse, the Yankee balloonist was startled to see a gray-colored Confederate balloon hovering nearby attempting to survey the Union defenses around Washington. The air contest was now no longer a one-sided race.

A month later, when the first serious fighting began at the battle of Bull Run, two Union balloons were in the air. An airship flown by veteran aeronaut John Wise accompanied the Federal army advancing on Manassas while Lowe's *Enterprise* patrolled above Washington to keep an eye out for a Rebel flank attack on the capital. Wise's balloon had very little impact on the battle since it was ripped open by overhanging trees when it was blown into an orchard near the battlefield, but Lowe's ship served an important duty on that day of disaster for the Union cause. When the defeated Federal army rushed in panic-stricken retreat back to the capital, Lincoln and his advisors were convinced that the victorious Rebels would be right behind in a march on Washington. However, Lowe pushed far into Virginia and telegraphed the president with the reassuring news that the Confederates were not pursuing the Yankees.

One part of the reorganization of the Union army after Bull Run was the organization of a Federal

Aeronautic Corps, the earliest predecessor to the United States Air Force. Workers at the Philadelphia Navy Yard were soon working furiously to construct a balloon squadron. Fifty seamstresses used almost a mile of silk to fashion the first new airship, a 38-foot balloon christened the *Union,* capable of holding 32,000 cubic feet of gas and designed to carry four observers and an enormous supply of telegraph wire. The floor of the *Union* was specially fitted with sheet iron to deflect Rebel rifle bullets and by August 29, 1861, the first airship designed for combat operators was on a reconnaissance flight. As it flew over enemy territory Confederate rifles and cannons blasted away, but the airship returned unharmed. A few days later com-

The Civil War saw the first aircraft carriers in the United States Navy as ships were equipped to carry the large observation balloons.

manding general, George McClellan, went aloft for two hours with Lowe becoming the first field commander to see his army from the air. The general was so impressed that he urged the government to make an all out effort to construct additional balloons and by the next spring an impressive fleet was ready for action. When McClellan began a huge seaborne offensive into the peninsula of Virginia he had available eight airships—the *Enterprise, Union, Intrepid, Constitution, United States, Washington, Eagle,* and *Excelsior*—for air operations. As the Union army inched its way from Norfolk to Yorktown, McClellan even received the services of the world's first "aircraft carrier," the *George Washington Parke Custis.* The *Custis* was a barge fitted out with a steam tug for propulsion and was refitted with a wide oval deck that would hold balloons and a deckhouse at the stern which held a portable gas generator for refueling balloons before each patrol.

This campaign between Norfolk and Richmond in the spring and early summer of 1862 was probably the most intense period of air activity in any war until World War I. Not only were several Union airships flying reconnaissance flights, but the Confederates responded with two of their own balloons. Both of these Southern airships were fueled at the Richmond gas works, and while one was a dull cotton balloon of Confederate gray, the other had been constructed largely from silk garments donated by the ladies of Virginia and was a stunningly multicolored spectacle when it was launched. There is no record of the aeronauts of either Confederate or Union balloons firing at one another over the Virginia landscape, but aeronauts on both sides were frequently under fire and sometimes balloons were shot up pretty severely.

The importance of aerial reconnaissance to McClellan's army was most dramatically demon-

strated during the battle of Seven Pines (or Fair Oaks) on the last day of May of 1862. That morning, as Thaddeus Lowe took to the skies in the *Constitution*, the Confederate army was secretly moving to attack a portion of the Union army that was almost cut off from the main force of Yankees by a flooding Chickanominy River. Lowe suddenly spotted the Rebels pushing through the woods toward the endangered bluecoats and the aeronaut quickly telegraphed General McClellan that he was about to be attacked. The balloonist also emphasized that the key to the bat-

Professor Lowe taking the Intrepid *up for a crucial scouting mission.*

tle would be an unfinished bridge across the river which was the only spot where reinforcements could go across to help their comrades. After Lowe spent much of the day telegraphing vital reports of where the Confederates seemed to be massing for new attacks the *Constitution* ran low on gas. When the balloon touched down the aeronaut jumped out of the cab and went back aloft in the newly fueled *Intrepid* to continue his crucial scouting mission. By nightfall, Union reinforcements were swarming across the completed bridge and the Federal line held.

While the value of aerial reconnaissance had clearly been proven on this bloody day of battle, the Union "airforce" slowly receded into the background for the remainder of the Civil War. General McClellan and at least two of his subordinates who were the most enthusiastic supporters of an aeronautical corps were gone from the army by autumn; Lowe almost died from sickness and exhaustion and could only return briefly to the army before he permanently retired. Most of Lincoln's new commanders thought that a balloon corps was too exotic for the battlefield. However, during the Civil War the world received a clear message that in future battles, what happened above the ground might very well determine who would win on the ground.

VI

The Special Weapons War

Once it became clear to both Northern and Southern leaders that the Civil War was not going to be a contest that would be over in one or two battles, both sides began developing special weapons that might give their army an extra edge in the almost always evenly matched fighting. Many of these special weapons were actually the prototypes of 20th-century weapons, such as hand grenades, machine guns, and self-propelled artillery, and sometimes Civil War battles were eerie previews of the kind of fighting that would take place in World War I and World War II.

One of the most famous scenes of World War II is that of American and German soldiers tossing hand grenades at one another in hard fought battles. However, the "pineapples" and "potato mashers" of the 1940s had Civil War equivalents in an ingenious weapon called a Ketcham grenade. This device was a five-pound oblong shell equipped with a wooden tail and paper fins to help guide it straight when thrown. A plunger at the nose detonated the grenade when it

The volley gun was a fast-firing weapon that could discharge a long volley of bullets with one detonation.

hit the ground. Some versions of the Ketcham grenade even came with a strap or cord attached to a fuse which would be wrapped around the thrower's wrist. When the soldier threw the grenade, the cord went taut and pulled a pin, igniting the fuse as the weapon flew through the air. A device of this type could cause very heavy casualties if it exploded among a group of enemy attackers who were tightly packed together, and Confederate troops used these weapons with deadly results in the sieges of Vicksburg and Petersburg.

Another weapon that could stop a large number of enemy attackers was a form of "mechanical" or "machine" gun that would be a crucial weapon in the World Wars but already was being tested in early forms in the Civil War. Confederate armament experts developed an impressive fast-firing weapon called a volley gun which featured 144 parallel chambers arranged like a honeycomb inside the casing of a cannon-like weapon. A single percussion cap would discharge all the chambers at once, unleashing a lethal hail of bullets at bluecoat attackers. Southern troops defending the North Carolina coastline used this awe-

The Gatling gun was a fearsome weapon produced by the Union from the blueprints of a Southerner, Dr. Richard Gatling.

some weapon in several small-scale battles but Confederate factories were never able to produce enough volley guns to test their impact in large-scale engagements.

The Yankees countered this Rebel weapon with a new device called a requa battery in which 20 rifles were connected to one another along a horizontal plane with all the weapons set up to fire at the same time. But this requa battery took too long to reload after each firing and Federal ordnance experts shifted their interest to a more devastating weapon called the Gatling gun. Doctor Richard Gatling, who was already a fairly famous inventor by 1860, was able to develop a revolutionary weapon in which the loading, extracting bullets, and firing of the gun would be performed by automatic mechanisms in order to produce an enormous rate of fire. Gatling introduced a multiple-barreled gun that was nicknamed a "coffee grinder" and operated by a crankshaft which rotated all of the barrels until a fresh clip of bullets could be inserted as the magazine emptied. This fearsome

The 13-inch "dictator" mounted on a railroad flatcar could fire a 200-pound shell over two miles.

weapon could turn a small number of men into a miniature army if they had proper protection from enemy fire. Ironically, Gatling himself was a Southern sympathizer but early in the war the Union government seized the blueprints for the new weapon and Southern factories didn't have the equipment to produce the gun. Several batteries of Gatling guns were in service with the Northern army late in the war and the relatively few times they were used both Yankees and Rebels were awestruck by their effect.

A third early version of a 20th-century weapon used in the Civil War was the concept of self-propelled artillery. Just as more modern armies used the internal combustion engine to move large cannons around on roads, Civil War armaments experts experimented with using steampowered engines to move heavy artillery around on railroads. By the time the war in Virginia had turned into a siege operation around Richmond and Petersburg in 1864, the United States Military Railroad had developed an impressive rail network connecting the widespread camps of the Union armies. One of the features of this rail network was the introduction of huge, long-range, siege guns fastened to railroad flatcars that could then be moved quickly from various points to attack vulnerable Confederate positions. The most powerful of these propelled siege guns was called the "dictator." It was a huge, 13-inch Federal mortar which could fire a 200-pound shell well over two miles. The recoil on this cannon was so powerful that it would push its railroad car back as much as 12 feet every time it was fired. While this form of weapon was limited to use only in those parts of a battlefield that had railroad tracks it still provided a preview of the use of tanks and mobile guns in the next century.

A mine tunnel was dug under Fort Hill in an attempt to destroy its arsenal.

While all of these special weapons received considerable attention by the public during the Civil War, perhaps the most heavily publicized "high tech" device of the conflict was the use of mine tunnels packed with explosives and designed to blow the enemy's men and forts sky-high. Since tanks and aerial bombs were not yet available to blast "impregnable" fortifications to pieces, the next best option was to get at the enemy from below. The first highly publicized attempt to do this occurred during the decisive siege of Vicksburg, Mississippi, which was the key to the Union or Confederate control of the Mississippi River. When the Federal army of Ulysses S. Grant defeated the Confederates outside the city and chased the Rebels into the fortifications, the first two attempts to storm the defenses were thrown back. At this point several Union engineers convinced Grant to authorize a huge tunneling operation to get at the Confederates from below. For several weeks blue-coated soldiers worked in shifts of 150 men each, digging a trench that approached the front of the enemy lines. Then 300 soldiers with mining experience were brought in to begin construction of the actual tunnel. Finally, by the night of June 24, 1863, a tunnel four feet wide and five feet tall extended all the way to one of the most powerful of the Confederate forts. Just before dawn on June 25, 88 barrels of gunpowder containing over a ton of explosives blew the defenders' redoubt sky-high. But Yankee assault troops were slow to take advantage of the hole in the enemy lines and as bluecoats pushed through a six-foot-deep crater, graycoats began tossing dozens of hand grenades down on the attackers. While the operation finally had to be called off, almost immediately a new tunnel was begun with a target date of July 6 set for completion. But on July 4, two days before the explosives were to be set off,

This mine tunnel was built under Fort Sedgwick.

Confederate General John C. Pemberton surrendered the whole garrison of Vicksburg and no one ever found out if the second mine would have worked.

A year later, after Grant had taken charge of the war in Virginia, the Confederates under Robert E. Lee developed even more powerful fortifications than those at Vicksburg. The Union Army of the Potomac had hundreds of trained coal miners in its ranks, and one of their officers, Lieutenant Colonel Henry Pleasants of the 48th Pennsylvania Regiment proposed exploding 12,000 pounds of gunpowder under a key section of the Rebel lines. By late July of 1864 the miners had constructed an enormous 500-foot tunnel with two lateral chambers extending 75 feet from the main galley. However, while the tunnel itself was an engineering marvel, the actual assault plan was incredibly botched. First, only 8,000 of the 12,000 pounds of explosives determined to be needed were delivered to Pleasants. Then two brigades of African American troops, who had trained for weeks to lead the assault after the explosions, were put back to a supporting role while white troops who had received no training for the operation were put in their place.

At 4:45 A.M. on July 30, 1864, six separate fuses sparkled toward the huge stack of gunpowder barrels and an awesome explosion rocked the early morning air. The exploding gunpowder blew a hole 180 feet wide in the Confederate lines and created an enormous crater 60 feet wide and 25 feet deep. However, most of the first wave of attackers, who were supposed to go around the crater, wound up climbing into the huge ditch and stood there marveling at the power of the explosion. The initial contingent of white troops was eventually joined by the black regiments and soon thousands of bluecoats milled around the crater as the Confederates organized a counterattack. The Rebels soon occupied most of the ground around the rim of the crater while the Yankees were trapped on the bottom and the result was pure slaughter. Southern troops threw hand grenades and fired rifles into the increasingly panicky mass of bluecoats and by early afternoon over 4,000 Union troops were dead, wounded, or captured. One of the most spectacular special weapons of the war had initially worked perfectly, but the great victory expected by the Yankees had turned into an embarrassing disaster.

During the Civil War, both Confederates and Yankees were able to produce awesome new weapons and devices that were far ahead of their time. Both sections of the country contained many ingenious people who hoped that the weapons they were designing would help end the war more quickly and help their side come out victorious in the bloody struggle. When North and South were finally reunited, this ingenuity would help greatly in making the United States one of the leaders of the new technological revolution that would change the world.

Glossary

battery	A grouping of artillery pieces or an artillery unit within an army.
blockade	A military maneuver in which supply and information sources are cut off to a city or harbor.
blockade runner	A ship or person that tries to break through a blockade to bring supplies and information.
bluecoats	Term used for soldiers in the Northern Union army during the Civil War because of the color of their uniform.
breechloader	A rifle that could be loaded from the rear of the weapon allowing faster and safer loading.
Confederacy	The Southern states that seceded from the Union formed a new country called the Confederate States of America also called the Confederacy.
Confederate	A citizen of the Confederate States of America; a Southerner during the Civil War.
Federals	A name used for members of the Union.
flying fougasse	Weapon used during the Civil War consisting of a cannon ball placed inside of a barrel filled with stones. When the barrel was dropped off a wall it would explode shooting the stones in all directions.
frigate	A small warship propelled by sails.
graycoats	Term used for soldiers in the Southern Confederate army during the Civil War because of the color of their uniform.
ironclad	An armored naval vessel.
muzzleloader	A musket that was loaded by ramming a bullet down the front of a very long barrel.
Rebels	Term used for Southerners in the Civil War.

redoubt	A small temporary enclosed defensive work usually dug or erected around the perimeter of a defensive position.
rifled musket	A single-shot, muzzleloading rifle with grooves (rifling) in the barrel that propelled the bullet farther than a smooth bore musket.
siege	A military strategy usually against a city in which it is surrounded by enemy troops and all supply routes are cut off. Usually used to try to get a city to surrender.
smoothbore musket	A single-shot, muzzleloading rifle with a smooth surface on the inside.
Stars and Stripes	The flag of the United States.
Union	The United States of America.
Yankees	Term used for Northerners.

Further Reading

Campbell, R. Thomas. *The C.S.S. Hunley Confederate Submarine*. WhiteMane, PA, 1999.

Catton, Bruce. *Terrible Swift Sword*. Doubleday, NY, 1963.

Commager, Henry Steele. *The Blue and the Gray*. Fairfax Press, NY, 1950.

Cross, Wilbur. *Naval Battles and Heroes*. Golden Press, NY, 1960.

Millard, Joseph. *True Civil War Stories*. Fawcett Press, NY, 1961.

Stern, Philip. *Soldier Life in the Union and Confederate Armies.* Fawcett Press, 1961.

Websites About Secret Weapons in the Civil War

Civil War Artillery: www.cwartillery.org/artillery.html

The Gatling Gun:www-acalal.ria.army.mil/ACALA/sma/asa/aagatlin.htm#1862

The Hunley Web Site: members.aol.com/litespdcom

National Firearms Museum: nrahq.org/shooting/museum/themes.shtml

Index

INDEX

PHOTO CREDITS

Harper's Weekly: pp. 10, 12, 14, 19, 28, 29, 31, 32, 34, 40, 47, 49, 55; Joseph Bilby Collection: pp. 17, 41; Library of Congress: pp. 30, 36, 44, 57; National Archives: pp. 16, 26, 37, 52, 54; United States Army Military History Institute: pp. 18, 23